LEARN TO READ
WITH IMAGES

Reading Made Easy With
MY FRIEND & ME

By Barnaby Pollock

This is a work of fiction. Names, characters, places, and incidents either are the product of the author's imagination or are used fictitiously. Any resemblance to actual persons, living or dead, events, or locales is entirely coincidental.

First paperback edition December 2022

ISBN 9798370003967 (Paperback)

LearnWithImages@Outlook.com

Little student

I'm a little student
here in school.

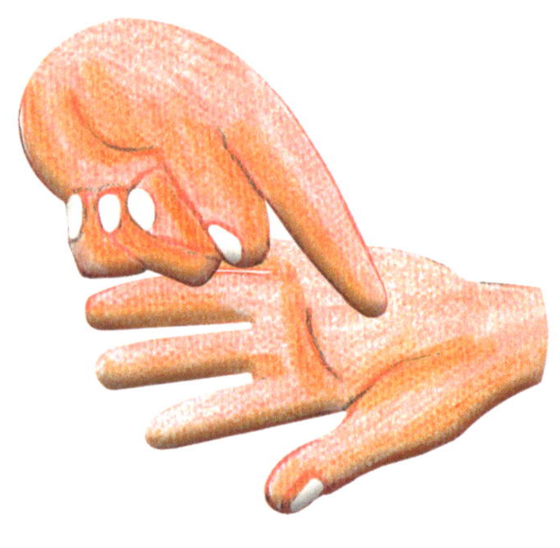 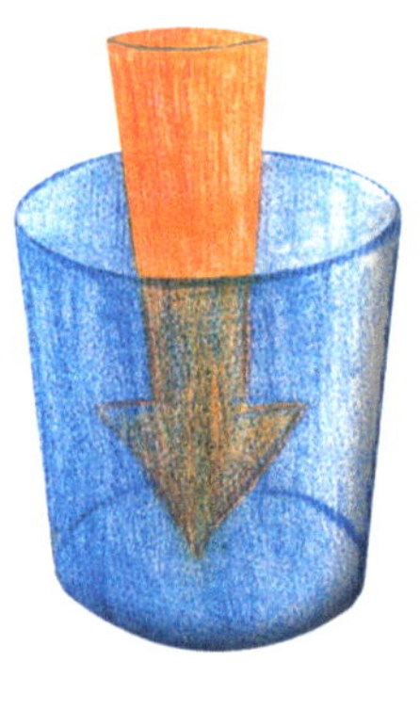 

She is my teacher,
she is cool!

  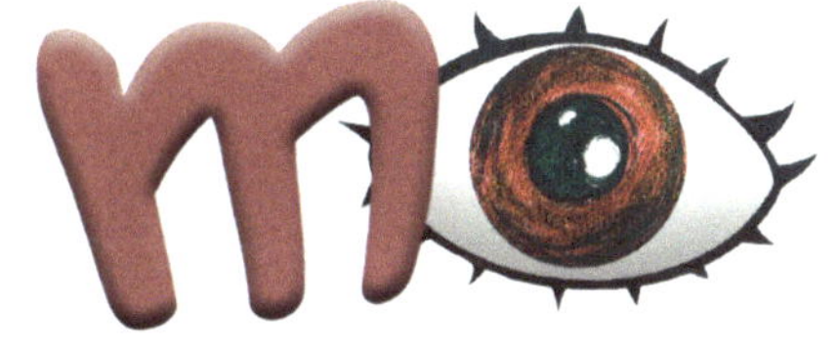

When I see it's
five o'clock...

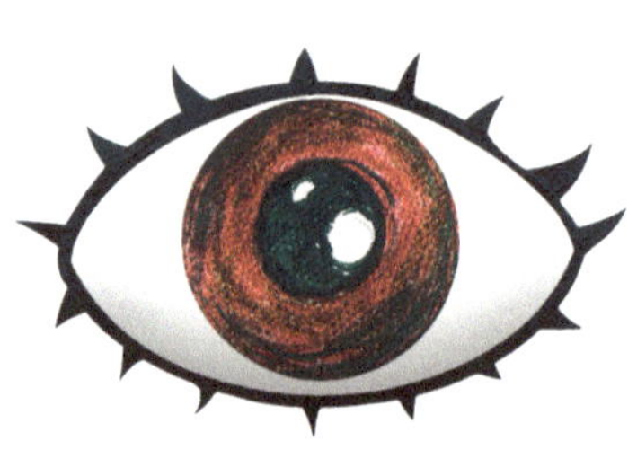

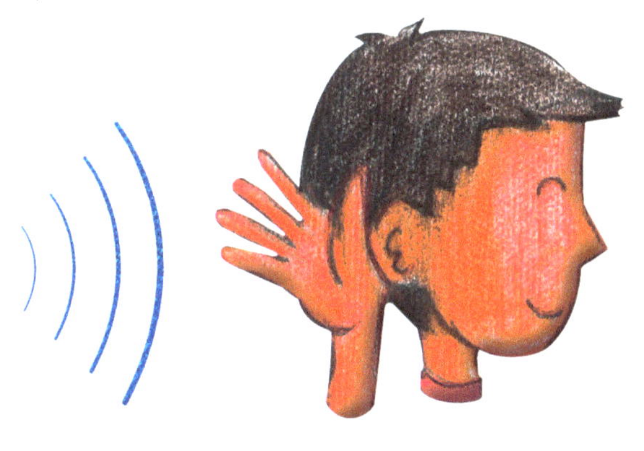

Hear me shout,
"Hey!"

Here comes mommy
to walk me out.

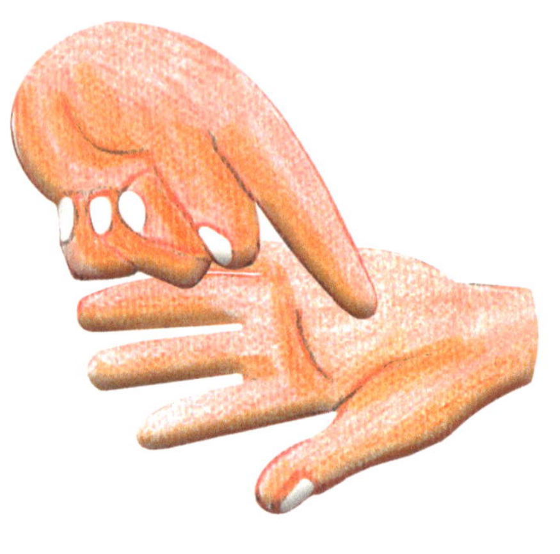

Playground

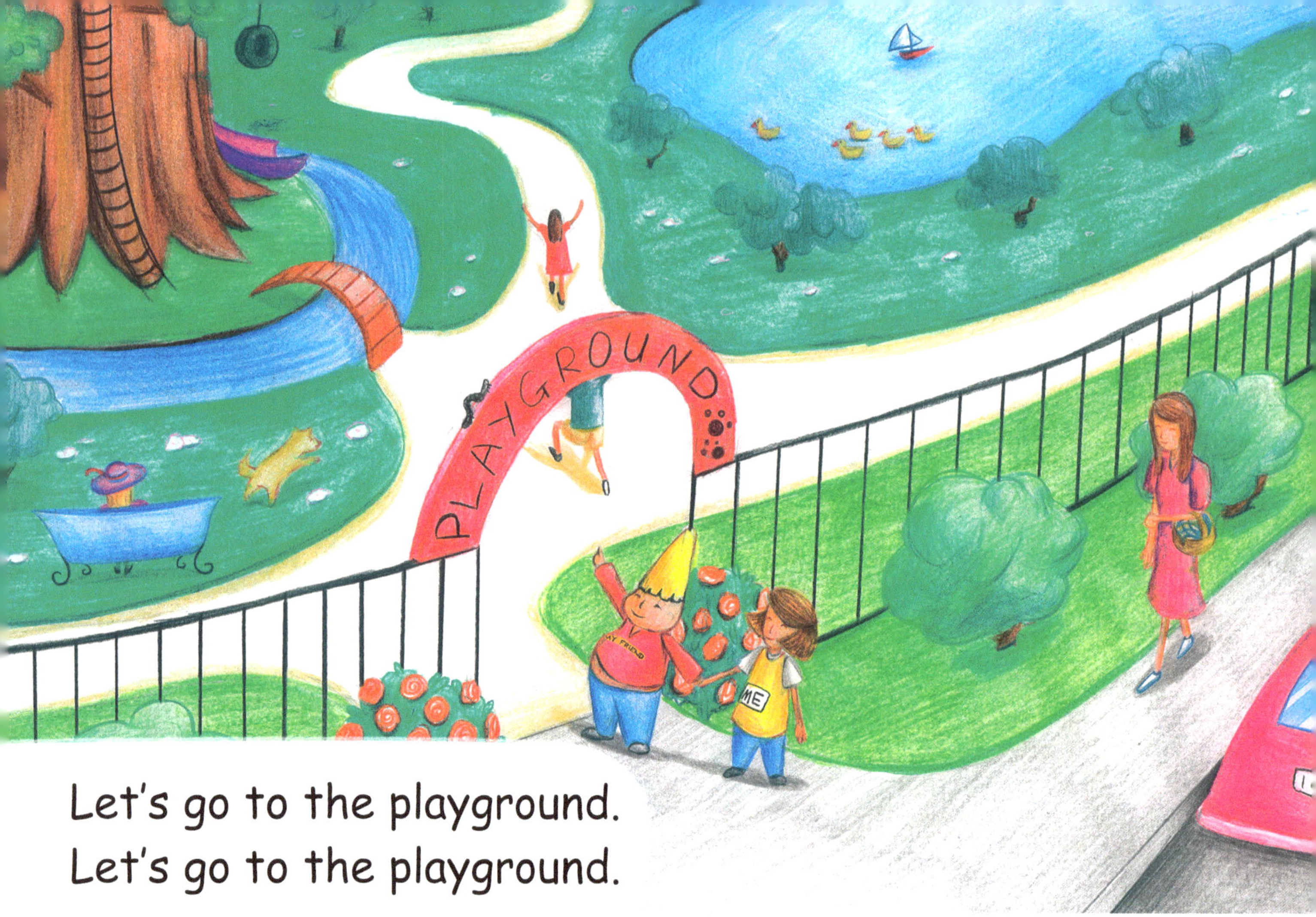

Let's go to the playground.
Let's go to the playground.

the

the

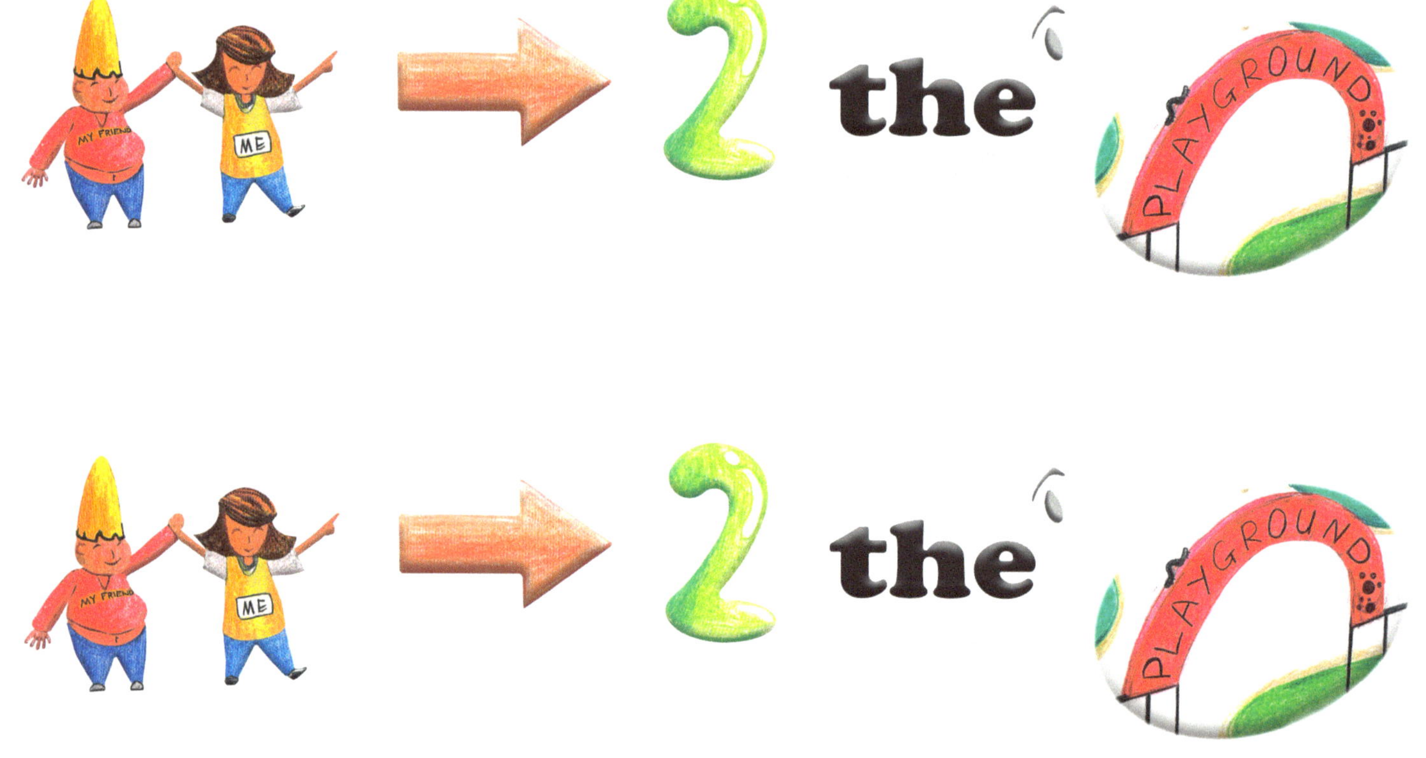

Climb up a tree,
up and down.

Slide down
the slide.

the

10

Swing on
the swing.

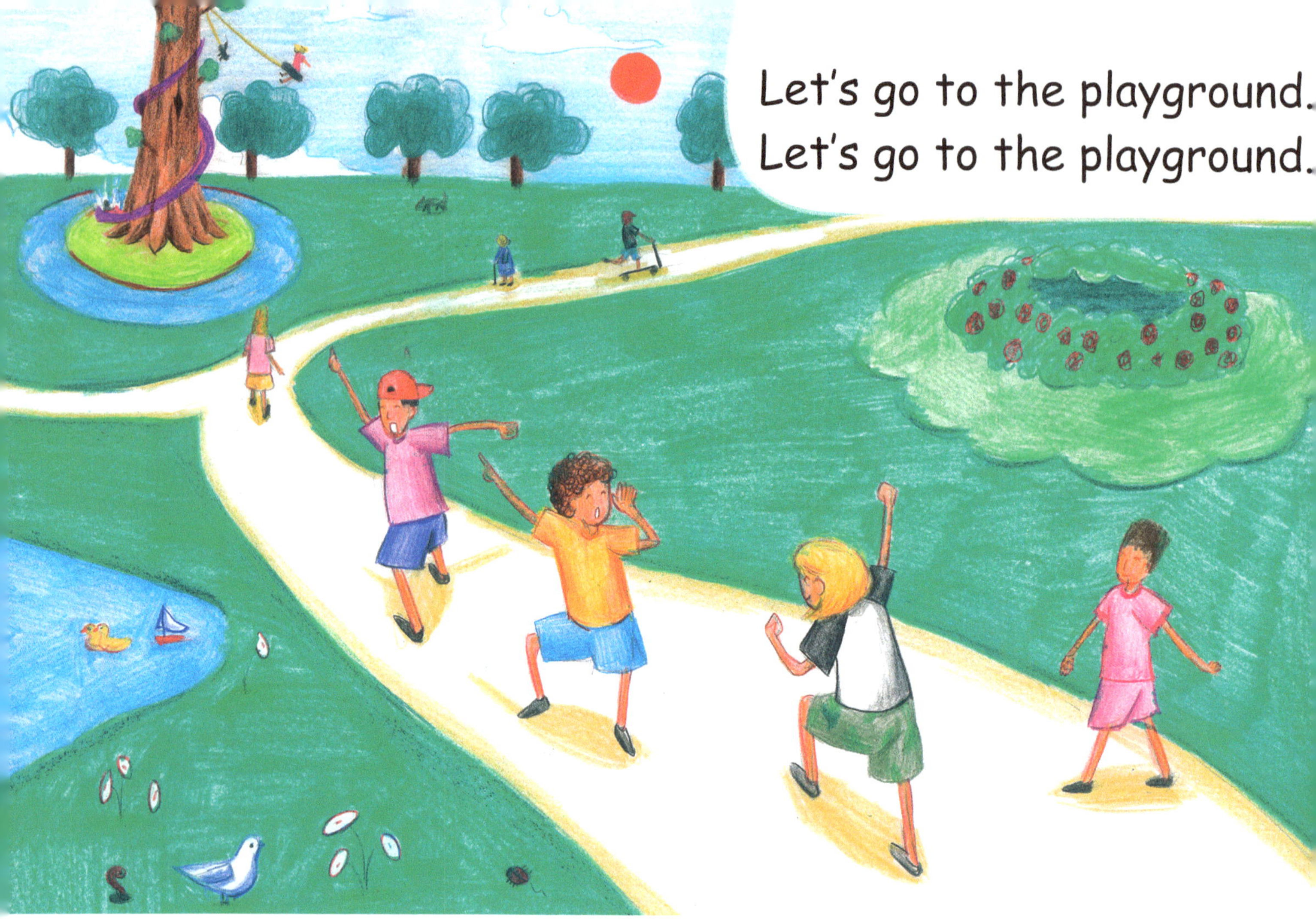

Let's go to the playground.
Let's go to the playground.

the

the

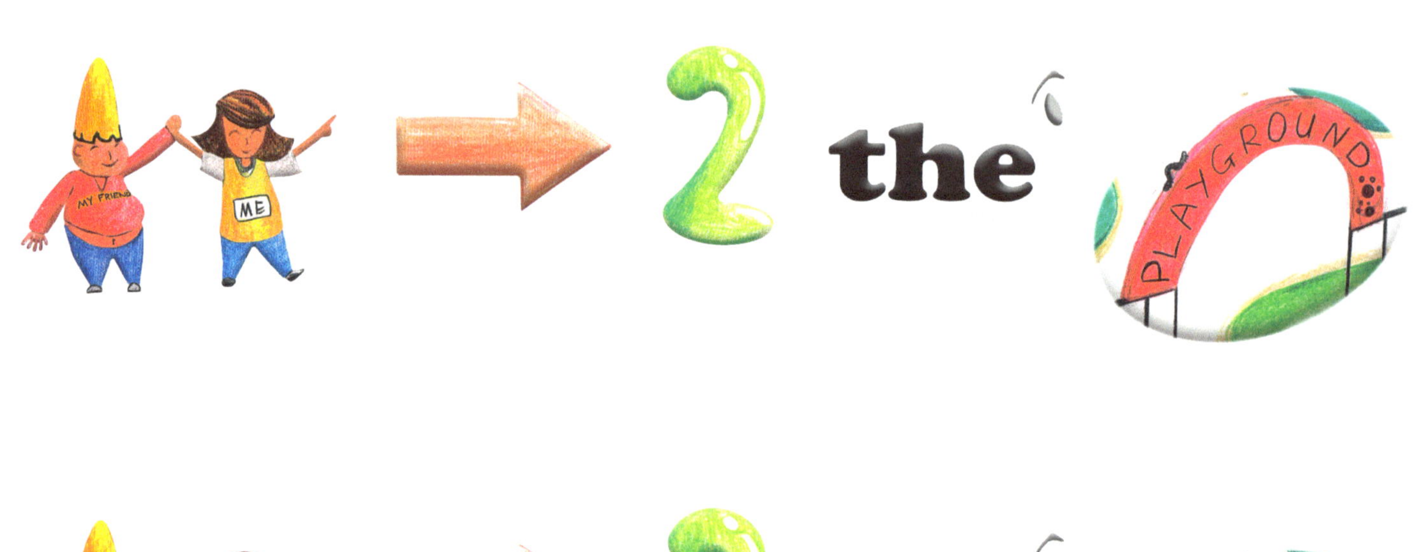

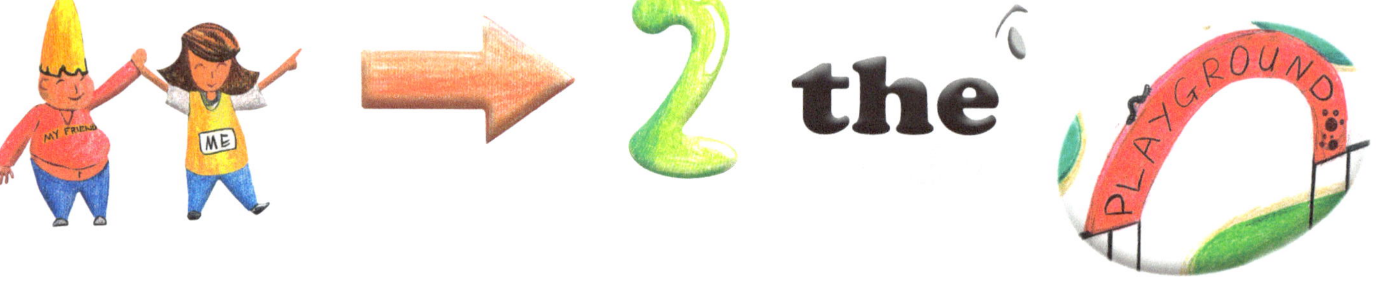

Everybody's happy playing on the playground.
the
PLAYGROUND

13

At school

I go to school
to learn to read.

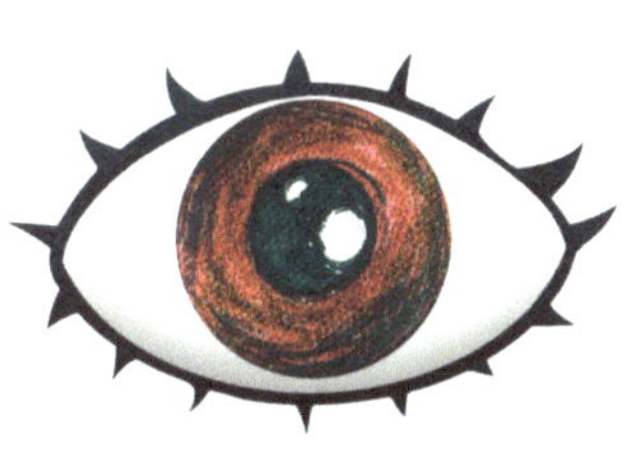 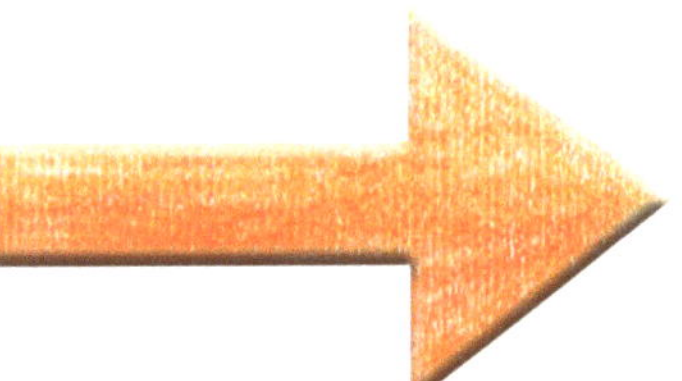 

Starting
A, B, C.

SCHOOL
I go to school
to learn to count.
123
cat
1+1
123

Starting
1, 2, 3.

I go to school
to learn to sing.
SCHOOL

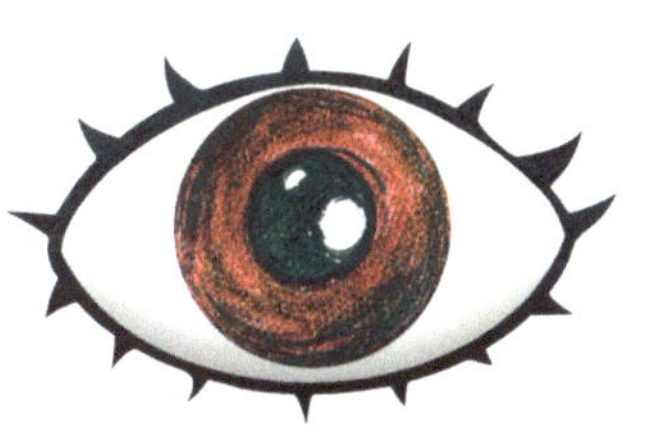

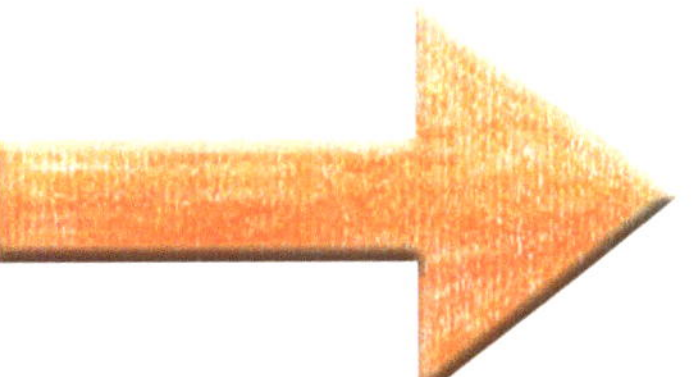

cat
1+1

shhhh~
Starting
doe, ray, me.
ting
ME

I go to school
to see my friends,

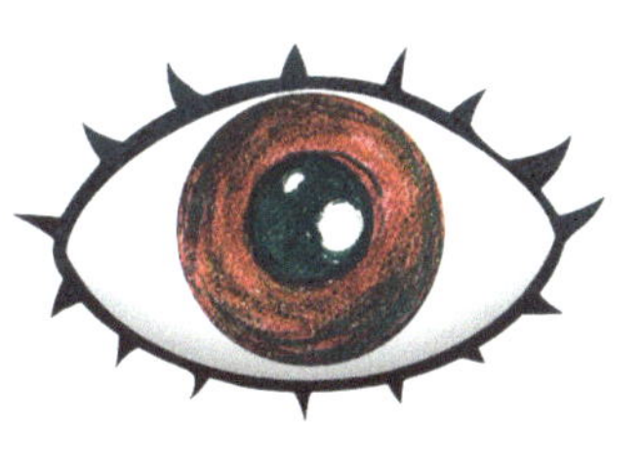
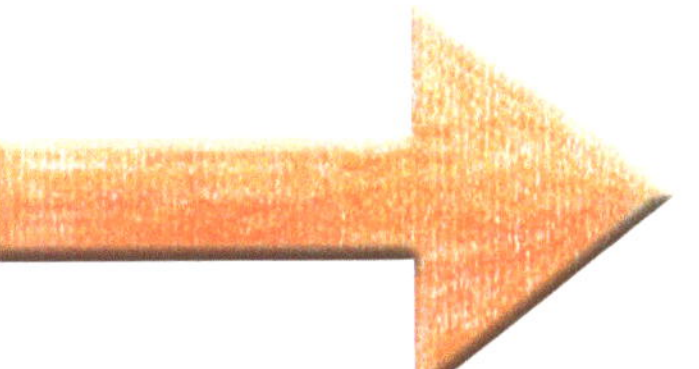

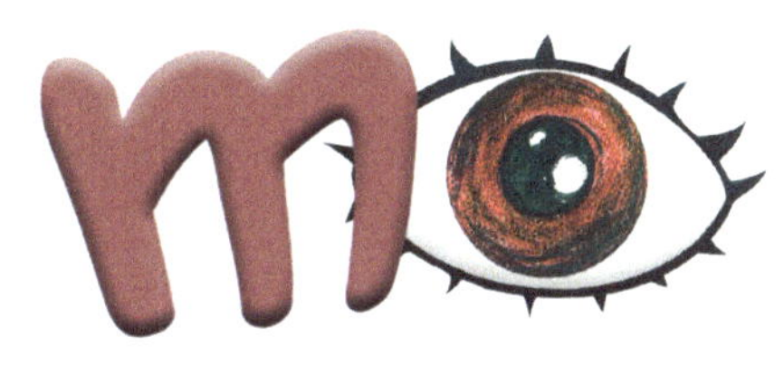

SCHOOL
and play
so happily!

At the lake

At the lake,
I can fish.

the

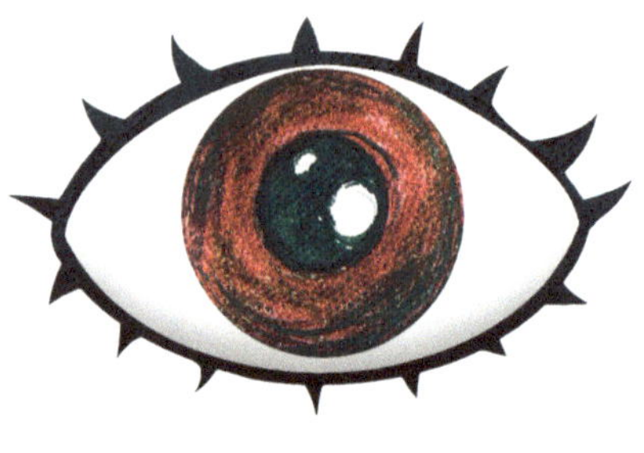

can

At the fair,
I can ride a
roller-coaster.

@  the 

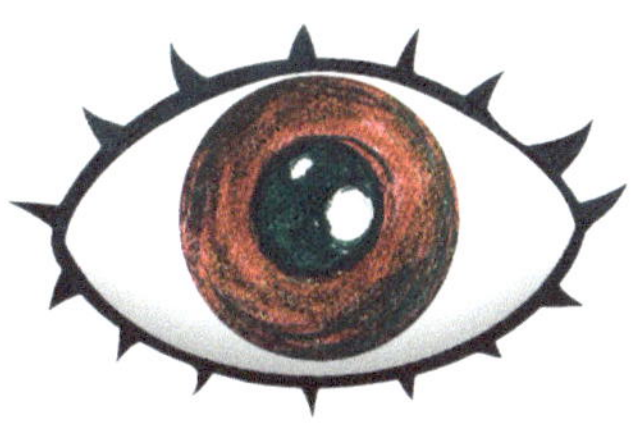  

A  

@ the

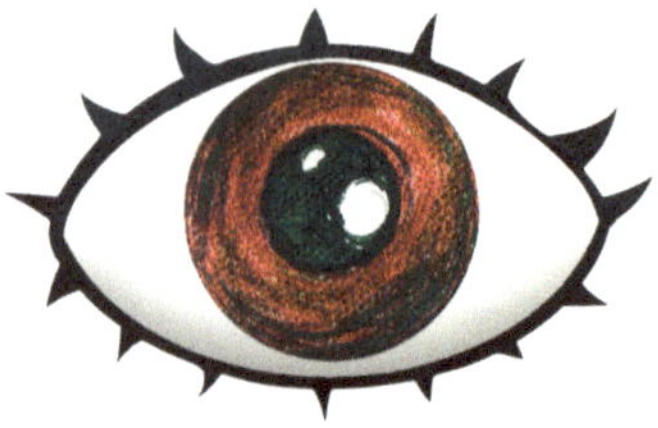

At the farm,
I can ride a horse.

@ the

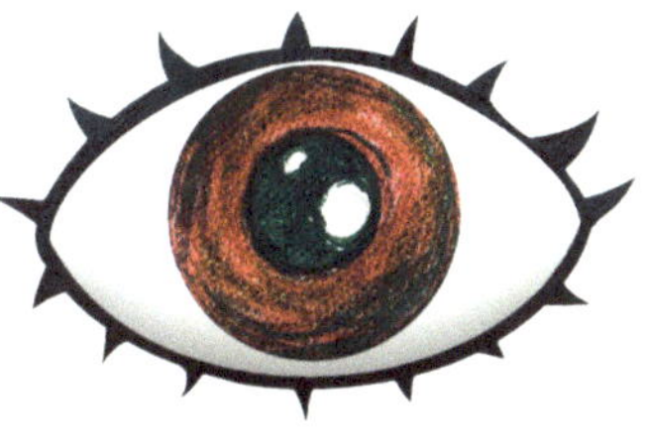

the

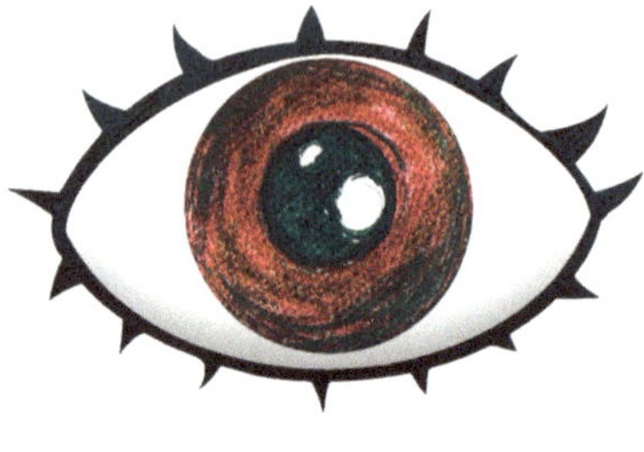

At the zoo,
I can see a lion.

 the 

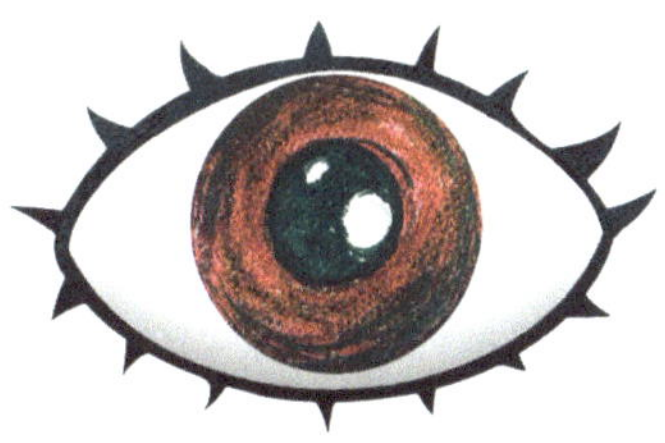 

At the beach,
I can make a
sandcastle.

@ the

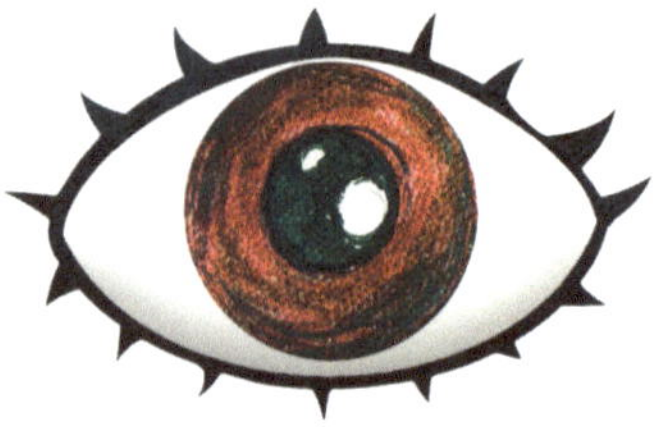

can

A

But at home,
I can go to sleep.

Vocabulary

A	a	(indef art)
	and	(conj)
	at	(prep)
B	beach	(n)
	but	(conj)
	buy	(v)
C	can	(modal v)
	cool	(adj)
	climb	(v)
	comes	(v)
	count	(v)
D	doe	(n)
	down	(adv)
F	fair	(n)
	fish	(v)
	friend(s)	(n)
	fruit	(n)
G	go	(v)
H	happy	(adj)
	happily	(adj)
	hear	(v)
	here	(adv)
	hey	(inter j)
	home	(n)
	horse	(n)
I	I	(pers pron)
	I'm	= I am (contraction)
	in	(adv part)
	is	(v)
	it's	= it is (contraction)
L	lake	(n)
	learn	(v)
	let's	= let us (contraction)
	little	(adj)
	lion	(n)
M	make	(v)
	market	(n)
	me	(pers pron)
	mommy	(n)
	my	(possess det)
O	o'clock	(n)
	out	(adv)
P	play	(v)
	playground	(n)
R	ray	(n)
	read	(v)
	ride	(v)
	roller coaster	(n)

S	sandcastle	(n)
	school	(n)
	see	(v)
	she	(pers pron)
	shout	(v)
	sleep	(v)
	sing	(v)
	so	(adv)
	slide	(v)&(n)
	start	(v)
	student	(n)
	swim	(v)
	swing	(v)&(n)
T	take	(v)
	teacher	(n)
	the	(def art)
	to	(prep)
	tree	(n)
U	up	(adv)
W	walk	(v)
Z	zoo	(n)

Little Student Song

Playground Song

I Go To School Song

I Go To School Song

At The Lake Song

At The Lake Song

Learn to Read with Images: An Introduction

Learn to Read with Images is a creative educational resource designed to make reading easier and more visually engaging. The philosophy is simple, effective, and suitable for learners of any age. This self-paced learning and teaching tool is highly convenient for use at home or in the classroom. It is targeted at beginner readers and is also beneficial to ESL and visual learners who struggle with literacy and breaking down phonics patterns.

Progressive Reading Levels

Learn to Read with Images is the key to unlocking each child's reading potential. There are six levels, each containing four stories that progressively increase in difficulty. Each level uses rhyme, sentence patterns, and elements of compound learning. The colorful, age-appropriate 'learning images' help early readers 'see' the words so they can connect the image to a word, and then easily decode (sound them out). By engaging more deeply with the content, readers can make quick connections, which aid significantly with vocabulary retention and memorization.

How Does *Learn to Read with Images* Work?

Learn to Read with Images is a simple, two-part learning process, as shown below.

- The upper half of each page tells a story and provides a visual environment for children to use their imagination.
- The bottom half of each page uses 'learning images' to represent the words in the story and helps with the pronunciation of more complex words.

Sight words that appear frequently are represented as 'text on a cloud' to help the students memorize words when it's time to read without the aid of the 'learning images.' This creative approach helps keep children interested so they can concentrate on learning vocabulary and fluency.

How Can You Use *Learn to Read with Images?*
It's as easy as 1-2-3!

1) As with any story, begin by reading to children, using the illustrations to help tell the story and spark their imagination.

2) Point to the 'learning images' as you pronounce each word. It is important that children learn to point to the words too, so urge them to point along with you as soon as possible. Help cement their recognition of the 'learning images' by repeatedly asking what it says.

3) Take time between pages to develop recognition of the 'learning images' by asking children to point at particular words and pronounce them. While they are not yet reading the written word, this is the first step in learning to read, which is exciting for everyone!

How Can Readers Build Confidence?

Begin with an easy 'learning image', like an eye. Keep in mind that 'learning images' are a visual tool to help make a connection between the image, its pronunciation, and the written form of the word. For example, the image of an eye is used to phonetically represent the word 'I', as well as 'eye', the actual word itself.

These regular prompts are important to ensure that children are learning to recognize the 'learning images' and not just memorizing words or sentences.

How Do You Know Readers Are Ready for the Next Level of *Learn to Read with Images?*

Once readers can correctly identify a word and its connection to the 'learning image', they are ready for the next level of *Learn to Read with Images*. There are several sight words in the text. For younger children, it is recommended to count the number of words in the text (upper half of the page) and do the same for the 'learning images' (bottom half of the page). This is a useful prompt to remind children that not all words in the text are connected to a 'learning image', and therefore, they must read from memory. As children move up the levels, they will recognize and strengthen their recognition of words, making them more fluent readers.

www.ingramcontent.com/pod-product-compliance
Lightning Source LLC
Chambersburg PA
CBHW042100110726
48006CB00002B/464

9 798370 003967